FULL THROTTLE

SPORTS CARS

BY THOMAS K. ADAMSON

EPIC

BELLWETHER MEDIA • MINNEAPOLIS, MN

EPIC BOOKS are no ordinary books. They burst with intense action, high-speed heroics, and shadows of the unknown. Are you ready for an Epic adventure?

This edition first published in 2019 by Bellwether Media, Inc.

No part of this publication may be reproduced in whole or in part without written permission of the publisher. For information regarding permission, write to Bellwether Media, Inc., Attention: Permissions Department, 6012 Blue Circle Drive, Minnetonka, MN 55343.

Library of Congress Cataloging-in-Publication Data

Names: Adamson, Thomas K., 1970- author.
Title: Sports Cars / by Thomas K. Adamson.
Description: Minneapolis, MN : Bellwether Media, Inc., 2019. | Series: Epic. Full Throttle |
   Includes bibliographical references and index. | Audience: Ages 7-12.
Identifiers: LCCN 2018031912 (print) | LCCN 2018033458 (ebook) |
   ISBN 9781681036588 (ebook) | ISBN 9781626179349 (hardcover : alk. paper)
Subjects: LCSH: Sports cars–Juvenile literature.
Classification: LCC TL236 (ebook) | LCC TL236 .A33 2019 (print) | DDC 629.222/1–dc23
LC record available at https://lccn.loc.gov/2018031912

Editor: Christina Leaf   Designer: Jeffrey Kollock

Printed in the United States of America, North Mankato, MN

TABLE OF CONTENTS

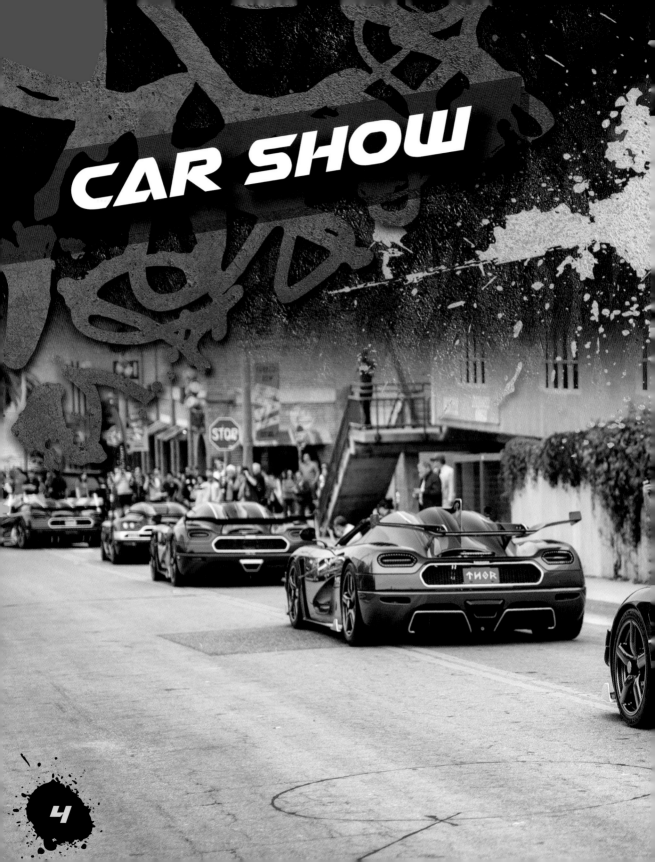

CAR SHOW

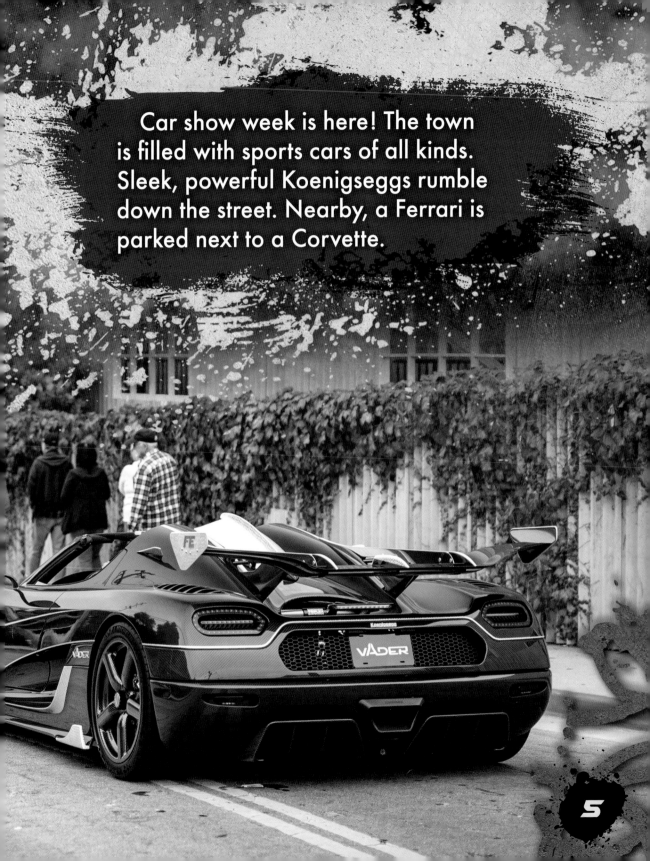

Car show week is here! The town is filled with sports cars of all kinds. Sleek, powerful Koenigseggs rumble down the street. Nearby, a Ferrari is parked next to a Corvette.

Visitors spot a **vintage** Porsche next to a newer model. These sports cars are loaded with **style** and **luxury**.

SUPER QUICK

The 2019 Corvette ZR1 can move fast! It reaches 60 miles (97 kilometers) per hour in 2.85 seconds.

The **high-performance** machines are a thrill to drive!

WHAT ARE SPORTS CARS?

HOW FAST?

The Koenigsegg Agera RS is the fastest car on the road. It has hit 277.9 miles (447.2 kilometers) per hour. But good luck finding one. Only 25 were made!

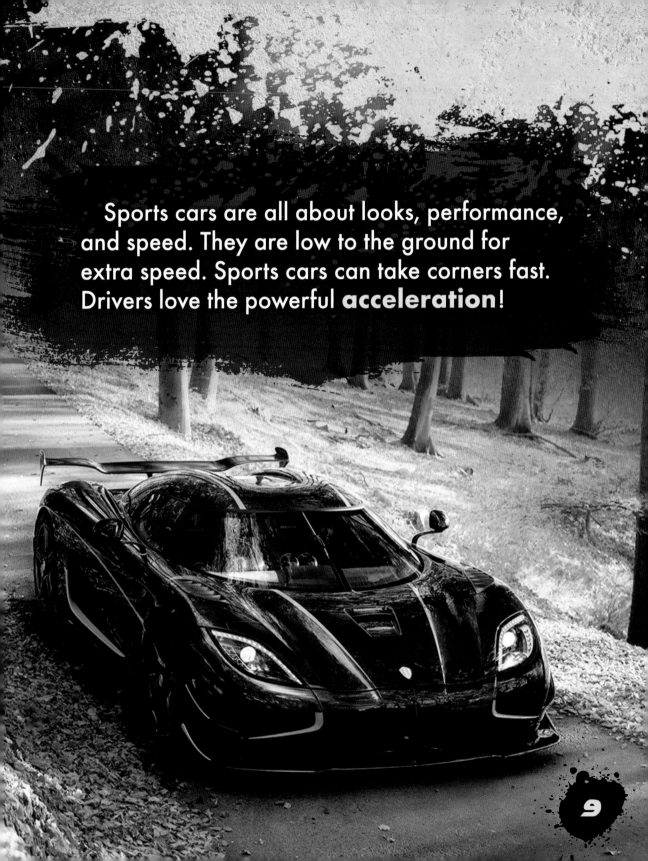

Sports cars are all about looks, performance, and speed. They are low to the ground for extra speed. Sports cars can take corners fast. Drivers love the powerful **acceleration**!

Most sports cars are **coupes** with two seats. These small, fast cars are great for hitting the road.

coupe

COOL DOORS

Lamborghinis have famous scissor doors. They swing upward to open.

Others feature big, powerful engines. Many sports cars have luxury seats and touch screens.

THE HISTORY OF SPORTS CARS

Fast luxury cars were a trend in Europe during the 1920s. They became popular in the United States after World War II. In the 1950s, many people had extra money. They wanted fast, modern cars!

1920s Rolls-Royce

AN AMERICAN CLASSIC

The 1955 Ford Thunderbird was an early favorite. It was one of the first top-selling U.S. sports cars!

SPORTS CAR TIMELINE

1963

Porsche 911 is introduced

1960s

Lamborghini begins building sports cars

1953

Chevrolet builds the first Corvette

2006

The Tesla Roadster electric car is introduced

1992

The Dodge Viper is introduced with a powerful V-10 engine

Styles changed over time. Sports cars showed off the latest designs and **technology**. In 2006, Tesla introduced an all-electric sports car. Today, carmakers use sports cars for their most creative ideas.

SPORTS CAR PARTS

spoiler

RACE CAR PARTS

The Ferrari 488 Spider has a double spoiler. This part is based on Formula 1 race cars.

Sports cars are built to be **aerodynamic**. They cut through the air at high speeds. **Spoilers** help airflow and push the cars to the ground. This improves the cars' **handling**.

air intakes

Sports cars have powerful engines. **Air intakes** add more power. They bring more air in and cool the engines.

Waste gases leave the cars through tailpipes. Some sports cars have four tailpipes!

IDENTIFY A SPORTS CAR

powerful engine

spoiler

tailpipes

air intake

tires

SPORTS CAR COMPETITIONS

Motor Trend magazine awards the Driver's Car of the Year. Experts test-drive cars on a closed highway.

CAR OF THE YEAR WINNER

The 2017 winner was the Ferrari 488 GTB. It costs around $250,000!

They do not look for the best value or fastest car. They choose a powerful car that is fun to drive!

GLOSSARY

acceleration—the act of getting faster

aerodynamic—designed to move through the air quickly and easily

air intakes—openings for air to enter the engine for added power and cooling

coupes—two-door cars with seating for only two people

handling—the way something is controlled or is dealt with; sports cars need good handling to make easy turns.

high-performance—better, faster, or more efficient than others

luxury—something that is expensive and very comfortable

spoilers—parts that help with airflow; a spoiler helps push the car down onto the road for better control.

style—a way of expressing oneself

technology—the use of science and engineering to do practical things

vintage—old but in good condition and valuable

TO LEARN MORE

AT THE LIBRARY

Doeden, Matt. *Sports Cars*. North Mankato, Minn.: Capstone Press, 2019.

Goldsworthy, Steve. *Scorching Supercars*. North Mankato, Minn.: Capstone Press, 2015.

Lanier, Wendy Hinote. *Sports Cars*. Lake Elmo, Minn.: Focus Readers, 2017.

ON THE WEB

FACTSURFER

Factsurfer.com gives you a safe, fun way to find more information.

1. Go to www.factsurfer.com.

2. Enter "sports cars" into the search box.

3. Click the "Surf" button and select your book cover to see a list of related web sites.

INDEX